This body was never made

poems by

Tara Propper

Finishing Line Press
Georgetown, Kentucky

This body was never made

ACKNOWLEDGMENTS

I would like to acknowledge my brother, Charles David Propper, for whom
this collection of poetry is dedicated. While this collection captures the grief
process, it also charts a path for overcoming and transformation. Charles, you
have taught me how to use art to explore, capture, and even perfect our lived
experiences, from the simple and mundane to the complex and tragic. Rest in
peace, my dear brother and friend.

Thank you to the following literary journals who have supported my work.
Individual poems in this collection have been previously published in the
following journals:

The Southampton Review
P-Queue
Moveable Type
Janus Unbound
Literature Today
Ekstasis Magazine
Taj Mahal Review

Publisher: Leah Huete de Maines
Editor: Christen Kincaid
Cover Art: Matthew Steven Kelly
Author Photo: Matthew Steven Kelly
Cover Design: Elizabeth Maines McCleavy

Order online: www.finishinglinepress.com
also available on amazon.com

Author inquiries and mail orders:
Finishing Line Press
PO Box 1626
Georgetown, Kentucky 40324
USA

Contents

Section One—Maternity Ward

Sea to See

The suitcase is turned off
Although there are stories knitted
into its velvet, the day laborers
have gone to sea,
the garbage smell resting at bay.

Where are you wild-wide eyes?
Has the dust taken my remains?
Or has the nesting night brought you in?

With sand-steady hands, I capture your sheep-
skin shores like a conch sounding salty morning.
With sandy hands I capture you,
treasured deep down the horizon's glut.

There is pounding beneath: awaken now, awaken
It's your time to carry the names through slanted hallways.

Mandelbrot Set

There are no more angles for you to disseminate
all over that convex beneath you

Share it and do no more
Do not take its life

Do not tell it your vulnerabilities
It does not care

There is nothing mother-proud
in the morning—her maternity

is reproduction, not production
Wash your hands before you land

and take only territor
Do not take space

Maternity Ward

There is a warm darkness that loves like wanting
She made sure to keep it close like cloves

When you shrugged from two sunsets passed
she regretted her monthly, regretted the pin-needle pain

of needing, of unconditional love. There was no baby, no sick
no sick potential. The sound from the hallway says

closeness. The baby-wallpaper uses loses its grip.
The sound from the hallway says nothing is as hollow

as empty. The wine-deep blooms collect like bruises.
Nothing wakes inside.

Back Brace

The huddled vertebrae bracket themselves,
warding incursion, knotting the spine,
and I am slender supine
in my bone-colored
brace, skin seams callousing, form colluding
against shape.

The back aches for the exactitude
of even shoulders and legs—a reclamation
of balance. The genius of 90 degrees
flush flat against a chair's back—against the squeeze
of constraint.
Like a saint, I am beyond bodily.

I have transubstantiated
from C-curve to X-Axis
from mass to matter
from filament to fiber
and there is no purity, only exoneration,
only enamel-laden reformation.

Hermeneutics

1.
Bobbing for baptisms
and the set down
rage. Give it a new age.

Give it your first born and your hell.

2.
She's a volcano volta turn
your cheek over
the hands need aim
and your face,
it is already hers.

3.
When upright up-and-goes as your father
once told of your mother
there is no evil empire
except her
rorschach rumble.

4.
That girl is tangle
in your hair. She's grilling
from the gill. She's marrow-heavy
in marrow color
.

Keep your Amens tucked under
they can't be for real
5.
Eyes blued in the halide heat
The tank reef closes shut as a hermit's
nesting.
This is what life is made of—
nature laden

6.

It's morning
and she's blushing
at the seams. There you are
boxing shadows.

This body was never made

for baby carrying
for plump blessings
for round

Instead it makes hard
angles and rectitude
It needs and needs

knuckled knowing
like piano keys that hurt
for fingers, searching for bone-

colored brahms. When I see them,
pink pulp, I am as a voyeur, watching
without feeling

I love so much in this world
but the tender edge of me says
there is nothing more here

to take

To a Statue of Mary (7:45PM)

I've made you over,
removed the white sheets
from your eyes, the placid nose

just doesn't fit the time.
When I am younger, I wait
for you to make me solipsistic,

rosary-like, an oracle of perfumery.
Now the jet-black performance
clogs the veins. I've spent half

a decade slicing it out, the clunky
rhapsody of ash. In a few months,
I'll be cleaner for it.

And there you'll be being,
stolid and ceramic, the cornea
of femininity. The evening

measures your service with bent
light and I've laid out six
pinecones to measure my own.

You're in your pallid,
again. I am not
going to pray today.

Benediction

What is my non-contingent
cause of contingency, the shelving carrying
our memory, causing fingers down back
of outstretched wall, like six candles awaiting -
the death of her
is always within him, sticky sick brother,
the candles causing the loss
of him, six outstretched
nails down back, she is his wonderful curvature,
she is his sticky sick
body cresting like upside-down shelving, the death
of him within her like shaky candles
carrying our contingency, the outstretched hand is a wall
of loss, of her, she was always awaiting,
of her, she was never awaiting.

Because He Said So

Every father deserves
to be a grandfather. There are blades

fatter than that girl.
Loss is maternal, without

it sacrifice means nothing.
Eat the fat, take the ash, he says.

When can I feel the stomach, he says.
She says: Only a mother knows

the sad dark within
It is Sunday groping

Wine spilt all over.
Something sick within.

Nocturnes, Op. 9 No. 1

There is beauty along
the river rot
Chopin's watercolor

ribboning within,
undoing time's finite.
Chopin's watercolor calls

like weeping.
The nailed-in reeds
close like contrition,

martyred mysteries,
everlasting underneath
the earth's heat.

It is the space
where mothers and sons
return to nocturne,

training their eyes
to see beneath
each parable.

Seascape at 4:42 PM

A faulty horizon line guesses
which side of sun
it possesses.

The sea gives no boundaries,
but doesn't offer itself
in any real way.

One chiseled cloud makes a metonymy
of itself. Cotton mammals lurk above,
both pure and untrue.

4:43 PM drops
its un-blessings. It's the ugliest of day—
and most aware.

Section Two—Sister Striations

Dear Brother

I'm looking for someone
to be sick with,
share suicides,
compare our art,
our little confidentialities.

I've made a habit of miscarrying
men. The last was no more god-
ready than you, Charlie,
charming as you were
in your butter-scotched rot,

me in my black pajamas.
We were dead together then
like ends split at the root,
ageless and elemental.
I cry,

an erosion of self.
The voice of you
stale as light

Testimony

The truth of her is not
perennial. The orderlies
maintain her with tools
and un-love. There is no need.

The trees care for none
of this, bending toward light.
And the nursing birds, tending
their stories, sink toward sun.

Everything's gone from me, now
The bed-sheets scroll sickness
And the holy roses need
something new to keep.

死   Shi

(pronunciation: \she\)

She's an open
wound in her
doctor's-office stirrups,
meticulous as a pentagram

She takes it an insult
they don't know her age
She's light enough
to float

She's alive, nevertheless
Her blood offends them
as suicide offends them
The mouth sees none of this

The mouth has learned restraint,
determined as an unholy god
Soon, she'll return to her kind--
the ladies with tubes

For now, they are looking
for scraps of her
baby. Every creator
must destroy something.

But the nurse-maids
feel nothing.
As the room
feels nothing.

To Muse

The reader and his tacky
stuck like faint expectation
She felt his doctorly, his need
There was nothing to quell the hermeneutic

There was nothing to keep the stuck
from his stealing. The book is sick
with nondisclosure
and dropping veils, like ladies on bent

legs. There was something in it, though,
wasn't I?
There was something like still life,
wasn't she?

And, the houses, full of her stories, are falling
like fallen women. Their windows cannot see
his burnt-out histories, hallowed along each
negative space. And there you are

behind open doors
kept gently
close like nighttime awaiting,
And there you are

like lines in a movie,
she could have said:
The ending is not
its meaning.

Heir

She took in bad air. It was tunnel vision. It was metallic. She
wanted it to stop. She wanted the breath to pass on like brother.

At seventeen, she only knew what things looked like. The
staircase said detectives, mother scream no, yellow air.

When the air went out, she couldn't feel time. She saw parts of
bodies that said *everything in time is loss*. She saw angularity.

When the air went out, she made time for knives.
The bad air yelled, "what have you done?" Dad didn't admit he

wanted solutions—wanted her to   not him to   .
The house was filled with barren. The breathe made her heavy

with bleach. The air loved this.
The bad air filtered through her into him. He drank it. She drank

it drank it up drank it too much drank
it fall down drank it sick drank it into new drink drinking to see

time lose its steady drank it in the
bathroom in the bedroom drank it like breath.

There was the bad air and the air they shared.
It wasn't bad.

When she thinks about time with him there isn't imperfect. The
wind sketches bloom. They retire unfocused.

Then family needed her. The family needed bulbous. The family
needed her to give air. She had only bad air.

The bad air wants her like life.
She gives it purpose.

Revolver

1.
You and your milky way toppers
like door jam knuckling its face
back together. Let the decay
decay.

2.
His ascetic pale
isn't the right tome for my skin tone.

Stupid Cupid,
I'm bigger than that rock-bottom bullet.

3.
I fancied a boy that sounded like brother
but was only a cover to smother
after doing it to myself and winning.

4.
Double your hedge bets
Nose to sternum is best bet for momma
and her angry maternity.
The pimp she let free had no musty lantern
only pills to suck on
until you're pop   pop   popping
your chest off
and *ohh, no,*
that suicidal has gone
and done it again.

Extinction

I am slowly extinguishing myself.
He knows and wants my sacrifice.
Tenderness is not a gift—tenderness
has never been a gift of mine.
The hostility of hands on elbows give and take
as a lung gives and takes breath,
each want resolution, each are a dysfunction.
The body is biblical in its distrust of women,
and in its angularity.
I hate all of its particularities.
It is evening now, and we lie
together, resenting one another.

Frederick Douglas

I am the most American
I am the most literary
woman

I see beauty in stone, in no-good land,
in Lincoln and Sylvia Plath,
marble-heavy, wine-heavy,

there is sickness in these bones.
My grandfather wept when we sang,
"Oh my papa, to me you are so wonderful."

My mother and father do not care
for Gettysburg, for Vicksburg,
they have lost their sons.

Yet, I cannot shake the Yankee-doodle
gush that rises every time I hear him,
Frederick Douglas.

I listen to every word.

God Principle

There are lines that throughout
forever tell of your love

They reach toward sun
Keep reaching my little big thing

There are so many oak edges to paint
you with. To shore you

up is like a bow pulling against time,
there is propitiation and peace

in every inch of your draw. Watch
when the day flowers root,

they are not dug in, only infinitely
blissful at the rain glow and mother-born

blades. They are swaying prayers.
Do not carry them tightly.

There is enough for full. And
the painting glass is still

from the inside. We gaze it
from outside.

The skin and bone not
completing.

Section Three—Floating Signifiers

Semiotics

This isn't going to be explicit
she said outnumbered
like barber's tongues and built up Brahms
like spoken spots and lots and lots of violence.
        Splayed legs hover over gifted china set with blue
autumn inscribed by dainty fingers.
        Does that makes sense?
        Make meaning for you?
Shall we meet as filaments do and bring out our boulders and
sound
the phoneme?
Did you need her when she took off her shirt and hurt?
I said I love you pulling the moon to my teeth
        and put down your bookish dear dear—
would you wrangle the wrought iron into clear
weather and weather this out for good fortune?
Would you reap June from grout—
allay the algae and gape logic-eyed
at fusty incantations?
        I am the only match that can dislodge of your dogma.
        Keep close and grow.

The Catch

The Benihana catch
you've sowed from knuckle sweat
soaks. It is conviction.
The face still letting on,
still unsettling death.

What a posture it takes
—mercurial and lithe as a double joint
or a baby's spine.
I do not want to sear its eyes
closed, disturb its rawness.

You say,
I'm a maudlin mourner,
clinching the catch
in your cooking chops
like some god particle.

But the fish, now half-mast,
defies rigor mortis.
It is the freshest
dead thing
I've prepared.

Domestic Reef

My clown is rabid for equality,
anenome-safe, she is a sententious
little proselytizer—a real sucker

The tank tells me my fortune in corals:
to the left, my past, a brotherhood of stony-
spined skeletons lean into their prehistoric

postures. The undead fossils scroll failed
resurrections into the sand as prophets do.
To my right, a leather, phallic and desperate

for my love. Above, my mother the halide
hates. She hates and elucidates with her calm
purple rhetoric—she doesn't age, she is

of a royal compound; she takes and consumes the reef
as a lens takes from history, eyeballing its insides
like some dead philosophy. Outside, I see only her

reflection.

Biorhetoric

I. At Home

On the sheet, your knees bent under chin
I say I am
ready; you uncurl
your fetal.

Morning charms don't penetrate.
We take coffee together.
Our kitchen literature says
everything alone is placeless.

It is November, and I am
betrayed by the cat-faced
spiders and their translucent
patterns—the season has taken them.

I carry the plates to their interment.
The dishwasher reveals its insides
like a pop-up book. It is November morning,
as you dial for the exterminator.

II. At the Parlor

Now that I have you
dead there'll be no more
stitch wounds to mend.
I am the only one here
at a loss.

III. At the Graveyard

I am not
looking for you.
The sky,

shapeless underneath its blue,
commits to the evening like saints
commit to the sick.

My breath keeps time. All week
I've hunted through grave lots,
ambitious and carrying offerings.

The clouds hold brittle
prayers by undistinguished gods.
The headstones fake death above

the season's pull with blank stares.
The names of the dead call and take
from me like sticky fortunes.

You call.
The stones of the self name the dead.
Outside, my feet chant to the stones

Backward Land

"she speaks spanish like
you, " he said, baptizing memories

in the kitchen. Summer self develops
like stories he wants to tell.

They are pedagogical and perpetual,
loving in both directions.

The texan evening brings
light like her, living long enough

to experience normality as anomaly.
Gulf streams across glossy grass,

collecting like painted portraits.
The sky has swallowed them

like deep-red afternoons.
And she's as lovely as children

waving, youth-misted.
They are remembering

to remember themselves
full-born.

Forgiveness

I am as if beneath
my stomach. The red war raw
is a lens. It does not
give nor does it
unfix the stitch
of lost brothers and losing
When you came to me
holding our small and lovely shells
I was a bruise. The platelets
collecting behind my injury.
The platelets bringing memory—
She was never a mother on Mondays
And I am no more a mother
than she—
To say this is to hurt
To say this is to undo hurt.
When you came to me carrying clippings
of baby hair, I believed
you, but wailing hope washes
these watering doors. The oceans
meeting between each bleached-out
beach. She is an ocean containing oceans
of wailing. I am she.
Will you forgive me tomorrow?
Say yes. Say yes, always.

Actus Purus

There goes the sun
groping the dark
for a cosmic
hero. She
has lost her
son.
Is it really the end,
my long lost?
There are vales of light
rooting inside,
too beautiful to be.
They are telling
how to mother
childless.

Two Portraits

(i)
There was dark in her
and the evening hated
each striation she mustered,
evening out past and present tenses.
Outnumbered, she let the numb root.

(ii)
You are in bed wheezing night sounds, future tenses rising.
I curl into you and subdue.
There is nothing in this room but shapes of us—amorphous
organs ascending and descending underneath the bed sheets.

Tara Propper earned her MFA in poetry from Stony Book University and PhD in English from the University of Pittsburgh. She is currently an Assistant Professor of English in the Department of Literature and Languages at the University of Texas at Tyler. As a poet and scholar, she is interested in the poetic and oft-ephemeral dimension of inhabitation and embodiment.

Her creative work engages with questions surrounding the feminine body, specifically issues related to how one embodies the feminine as a cultural identity. Moreover, her poetry also explores questions surrounding ancestral lineage, loss, and the relationship between space and representation. Hence, this collection of work synthesizes these twin concerns insofar as her poems undertake an ever-shifting perspective that seeks to recover individual and historical agency through a renegotiation with the environs of the past.

Tara Propper's research focuses on the relationship between literacy and identity, specifically the ways in which textual production can shape and impact how we define ourselves within and beyond a public sphere of representation. Her research investigates the concept of "the public" and what it means to write into or outside of this sphere. The ultimate aim of her scholarly and creative work is to examine how our local spheres of influence, including local material sites, local cultures, and community literacies influence our forms of communication. Moreover, her goal is to empower readers, writers, and students of writing to recognize the ways in which we can merge the rhetorical and poetic to create new opportunities for self-discovery, interpersonal communication, and community engagement.

Her poetry has appeared in the *Southampton Review, Janus Unbound, Literature Today, Ekstasis Magazine, Shuili Magazine, Taj Mahal International Literary Journal, Moveable Type, Vagabond City Press, and P-Queue. Her scholarly work has been published in Composition Forum, Dialogue: The Interdisciplinary Journal of Popular Culture and Pedagogy,* and *Resources for American Literary Study.* She is currently an Assistant Professor of English in the Department of Literature and Languages at the University of Texas at Tyler.